A Mosaic Of Color And Light

Poems based on the

haiku style by

Marshall Butch Armstrong

This book has been published
through Createspace and Kindle
Direct Publishing 2018

No part of this book may be
reproduced or used in any manner
without the written permission of
the author

ISBN-13: 978-0692100561
(Marshall Butch Armstrong)

ISBN-10: 0692100563

A Mosaic of Color and Light

Introduction

From my earliest memories, I have been a rule breaker. More often than not, this behavior got me into trouble. I never let it set me back however, because I also discovered new and interesting ways of doing things. So it is with writing haiku. Haiku was invented by the Japanese several centuries ago. It was devised by taking the first three lines from an earlier poetic form called, Renga, separating them and calling the new art form, haiku. The new form of artistic expression had rules (you can see where this is going). Haiku was written in three lines containing seventeen word sounds (onji). Five in the first line, seven in the second and five in the third line. (Originally haiku was written in a single line.) The haiku had to be written about nature. It had to contain a "season" word so the reader would know the setting for the poem. Two lines would be called a phrase and the third line would be a fragment. The fragment had to be separate from the phrase but connected poetically.

Which two lines were the phrase would be up to the poet. Haiku also contained "break" words that showed the separation of the phrase from the fragment. It had to be written in the present tense without simile or metaphor. And considering that these were not complete sentences, no punctuation or capitols were used. When haiku first started to be written in English, some of the rules were changed. English syllables are different from Japanese word sounds. So, a seventeen syllable haiku is different from a seventeen word sound haiku. As time progressed more rules were broken. Today's haiku are written by the rules and by breaking the rules. If it's not written by the rules, is it still haiku? I will leave that to your own judgement. When I started writing haiku, I wrote by the rules. I had to know the rules to understand haiku. I also needed to know the rules to break them properly. Believe me, it's logical. Since breaking rules seems to be my forte, haiku is right up my alley, as they say.

So, I hope you enjoy these haiku. You will find most of them are about nature as I find it much more interesting than most other things. They are not arranged in any particular order. You will find one about winter right next to one about summer. I don't want you to get too comfortable with a pattern. It's good to find yourself on the raggedy edge, as Captain Mal, of the spaceship Firefly might say. Hopefully you will gain an appreciation for the art of haiku and maybe try writing some of your own. Don't forget to break some rules.

Marshall Butch Armstrong 2018

always wind

from across the lake

frenzied flag

great blue heron

stalks its prey in silence

windblown cattails

sunlight on bare trees

sap runs free

to feed the ants

dew drops on grass
appear to be diamonds
shining with sunlight

cold still lake
a loon cries hauntingly
stopping to listen

cold fingers of fog
creep along the ground
and disappear

the wind blows

angry gray waves

on a distant shore

lichens on tree roots

beautiful colors

wet with spring rain

windblown evergreen

new trees from

lost pine cones

spider in moonlight

the web's deadly beauty

waiting for a fly

protecting the young

blackbird feigns a hurt wing

a convincing ploy

fresh turned earth

beneath my fingernails

the smell of spring

windblown wispy clouds

windblown wispy birds

fly against the sky

mid day delight

a tune forgotten

comes back

prairie grass

weaves and bends

the silence of strong wind

a kind word

a hand held

the silence of strength

giving hope

the world over

the silence of love

three male turkeys

spreading out their fans

asserting authority

sunset blue and orange

on a bare branch

a bluebird sings

from the lake

a haunting loon call

ghost of spring

white egret

the fish and water

are one

open your mind

to find the path

meditation

turkeys and geese

feed in the field

an eagle searching

this intersection

of sight and sound

a mind

a loon calls

black against gray water

early morning

a blue butterfly

hovering in the air

magical creature

red cardinal

against a backdrop of snow

sweet morning music

cardinals gathering

on a branch talk and sing

the air electric

fluffing their red wings

the color contrast of snow

and bright bird's beauty

suddenly flying

a chorus of sight and sound

one red bird remains

sitting alone

fluffing feathers

a sound of warming

brown dirt scooped up with

roots worms bugs and seeds

the feel of springtime

ancient pine

alone on a hillside

breathes

thunder and rain

the beauty of a spring storm

washes shore rocks clean

wildness in the woods

red bellied woodpeckers are

head banging today

dull gray sky

snow and cold

eternal winter

find who you are

empty thought from your mind

and see yourself there

thunder crashes

a storm rages through the night

dawning clear and bright

statue in water

suddenly moves swiftly

a white egret

snow falls wet

winters last ravaged death throes

make way for spring

flickering green light

fireflies play in the field

light up the night

a flower floating

on closer inspection

a butterfly flying

a common sparrow

taking a dust bath

fluttering movements

sunlight warms

a small creek

fish play

wind in the trees

speaks of things

better left unsaid

ancient willows

tossing out ideas

born on the wind

wind blows trees

and ripples water

a late evening

aspens waving

in high winds

stories to tell

geese fly

with long shadows

upon the ground

cars on the road

background noise

of daily life

dust floats in sunlight

among evergreens

lichens on gray bark

amber ice crystals

holding sunlight in my hands

falling away

four wings beat

a dragonfly breathes the fire

of an orange sun

shafts of light filter

through cracked window glass

a mouse chews a seed

rain on the pavement

filling cracks

rivers running

rain falls like tears

on a lonely world

washed clean

mourning what was

a funeral procession

rain in the graveyard

lightning flashes

bright and hot in a storm sky

cold rain and wind

cicadas whine

after a summer rain

shimmering heat

bare trees

a grandfather's ancient hands

reach for the sky

black crows

against gray skies

thoughts roaming free

an eagle soars

to great heights

becomes the sky

meteor streaking

fire in the sky

a sad leaving

the milky way

bright pathway of stars

darkens the night

big sky clouds and wind

across the horizon

birds carve a path

rain and lightning

crashing through a black sky

an orchestra

tumble in the sky

mating eagles fall

creating life

robin on a fence

announcing its opinion

to the world

leaves flutter and fall

as the squirrel ready's the nest

a cold breeze

first green points

of spring tulips push up

black soil

water trickles

in a stream between fields

bringing life and fish

lichens and moss

tree branches disappear

beneath

float plane

landing on the lake

brings news

fire spreads through trees

natural phenomenon

bringing new life

the people dance

to celebrate life

the way

water laps on sand

washing away the pain

and dirt of life

ghosts of past lives

haunt dreams of

silence and death

she touches his hand

over coffee and tears

saying goodbye

ground squirrels tumble

playing in the grass

games of youth

white egret

fishing for frogs in a pond

they jump to safety

an old house

holding memories and dust

a mouse stirs

dirt road

an old house at the end

empty for years

the cock crows morning

waking those within hearing

a new day

five turkey vultures

swirling around the sky

something died below

lightning forks blue white

in a treacherous storm sky

thunder rolls aloft

baby turtles

crawling through the sand

searching

a fish jumps high

streaming water through the air

jubilation

in silence

the pink and purple sunset

breathes

green heron

lunges for a frog

comes up empty

kingfisher dives

under the water

finds his dinner

under the lamppost

alone in the night

she is gone

dragonfly alights

on a gravestone

a life remembered

spreading her ashes

in places she's never been

memory endures

holding hands

a beautiful connection

forever

a familiar song

memories racing back

to another time

notes on the keyboard

coming together

a beautiful song

a kitten plays

with a ball of yarn

no tomorrow

a silver pen glides

across empty white paper

new words

find yourself

searching deep within

before you're gone

moonlight casts silver

shadows on snow and ice

surreal landscape

ancient path

well worn through the trees

an uncertain route

a single bell toll

calling the faithful

home

broken tree limbs

amid dry crumbling leaves

new buds on branches

a green heron

stabs at movement under water

misses the wily fish

cat stalking his prey

suddenly distracted

the mouse runs free

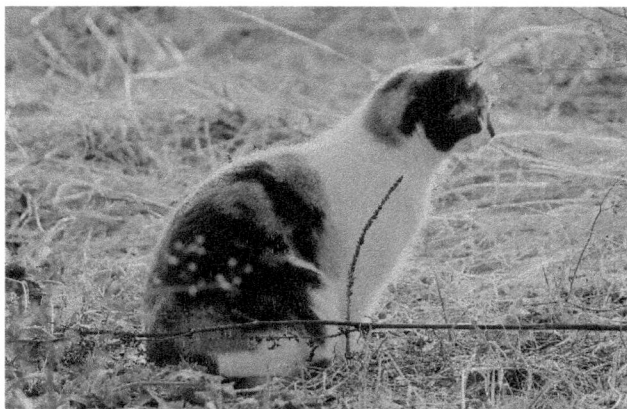

diving osprey

disappears under the water

rises like a phoenix

a dragonfly holds

the world in its glossy wings

and the universe

a thousand stars

light the mountain path

after the sun

summer heat

reflecting on water

shimmers the air

wind cools the day

beneath the cover of leaves

bright green brilliance

the cold north sea

empty but for ships

and monsters of the deep

insects buzzing

a cacophony of sound

night symphony

green scooter

gliding down the avenue

freedom on two wheels

cool night air

receives the crackling fire

swallowing it whole

wolves howling

heard from the dock

an eerie sound

fresh tracks

in the new fallen snow

tell a night tale

three quarter moon

rising over the pines

enlightening the path

a single duck sitting

beside the trail in the snow

waiting for spring

water laps at stones

a mosaic of color

and light

fluttering wings

spreading snow crystals

fruitless

in the graveyard

old bones resting

under spring flowers

the old windmill

no wind will move

rusted metal

yellow weeds grow

around the old well

long dry

snow drifts through

cracks in the old farmhouse

a door stands open

mice scurry

across an unpainted floor

abandoned shack

a swayback horse

chews grass in a field

in his time

a pile of stones

at the edge of a field

rising up

old fence posts and

barbed wire show an edge

an empty field

white bells

delicate flowers in green

perfume the air

unheated cabin

splashing cold water

fully awake now

tea sits cold

in a cracked cup

sorrow on her lips

hooded merganser

newly arrived on the river

with his mate

the geese return

only to find snow and cold

ice on the water

the old man's eyes

tell a tale of lost love

remembered

painting the sky

my brush across the canvas

is blue today

a misty morning

shadows glide across the sky

birds in quiet flight

lightning brings

the sound of thunder

summer storm

wet green fields

a light breeze

cleansing rain

mist over the fields

early morning sun

burns it away

forty shades of green

too much rain

the hay grows long

sunlight reflects

on ruffled water

wind in the trees

roosting in trees

web footed pelicans

water birds

stormy sky

rain and wind show

natural beauty

perchance to grasp

golden drops of the sun

in a deep winter

swallow builds

a nest on a tombstone

at home with the dead

green flash

phenomenon of sun

a rare sight

three squirrels

chasing in a tree

rituals

straw colored cattails

a barrier to sight

duck's refuge

the love of a child

always from the heart

in her smile

she moves

graceful in moonlight

she moves

the old woman

still twenty in her mind

dancing free

sheep graze

on a steep hillside

stone walls

a white deer

ghostly movement

through trees

dreams of sunshine

the air saturated

with rain

lightning bugs

beneath the crab apple tree

warm summer

chasing the devil

between the light and the dark

waiting for dawn

wind blows tattered thoughts

across a landscape of mind

still thinking out load

in this time of strife

laden with burdens

our loved one's woes

standing in snow

brown remnants of summer weeds

tremble in the wind

rain on the window

my dark mood etched in glass

storm tossed sea

dry grass crunching

under my tired feet

walking off the path

spider hanging on

a long silk thread

let's go and flies

in the morning light
of a cold winter day
coyote waits

sunlight through
a broken window
fractured time

pink wispy clouds
abide in a pale blue sky
forty-three degrees

rainfall in autumn

a drangonflies wet wings

buzz dry with flight

blood red moon

revealed in a starry sky

signs and portents

a stone wall

moss covered along the road

remembrance of home

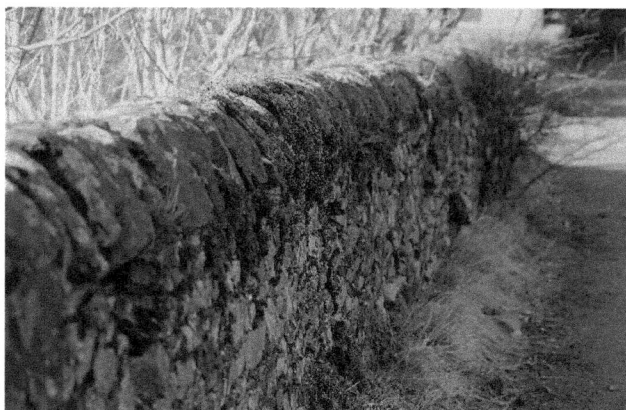

turning away

from the sorrow in their eyes

a refugee dream

lightning in the sky

a breeze ruffles the water

there will be rain

captured by the sky

held in place by a dream

her mind flows

rain on the road

creating a hazy mist

pretend fog

dead eyes of a child

stare accusingly

sand and saltwater

fog lingers

like remnants of a dream

barely remembered

cool of morning

gives way to summer heat

august thrives

in dark trees

owls sing to each other

a chorus of frogs

crows call a warning

dark sunflowers and gray mist

my morning walk

my life reflected

rain drops leave dirt trails

on the window

in healing yourself

mind and body harmony

an essential truth

hazy yellow sun

in a forest fire sky

gives little heat

coyotes howling

revealed in moonlight

I join in

autumn has its way

trees turn slowly

in a cold north wind

a loon laughs at

the lunacy of humans

floats away

thunder rolls

across a leaden sky

beautifully dark

swallows dive and swoop

teaching the young to fly

a crow intervenes

butterflies floating

in the hay field

sweet nectar

on a wet morning

the applause of aspens

I take a bow

moonlight on pines

ghostly images

against northern skies

reflecting my soul

water smooth as glass

an august moon

walking silently

a grass snake crosses my path

observe without judgement

clouds forming

mountains in the sky

white on white on blue

orange and black

flutters by

a butterfly

a murder of crows

entertaining dark thoughts

as am I

white butterflies

in the hay field

drink morning dew

snow falling

like thoughts in a dream

melting away

camera lens

reflecting what it sees

as truth

hummingbirds

buzzing at flowers

in and out

weary traveler

sleeping on a hillside

dreams of a hearth

blue and red parrots

on a green branch

in a painting

waiting

for snow to return

on a spring day

drums resound

playing to the beat

of your soul

facing off

the squirrel and the blackbird

who will win the branch

chessmen

stare from across the board

intent on war

ice out begins

revealing cold water

frozen in time

cows graze

in an empty field

geese protest

goldfinches

noisy at the feeder

nesting time

building beds

sunfish protect them

spawning life

on a cold morning

a kayak slips away

the drip of water

the mist on the lake

parts as the boat moves through

beautiful silence

red wing blackbird

nesting in cattails

calls a warning

snap of the shutter

camera gets a shot

of beauty

log cabin

painted many times

bare wood

a small stream

gurgles delightfully

I spread her ashes

the guitar solo

brings tears to my eyes

and his

shivaree

a celebration

at the cabin

skipping along the road

the irish red headed lass

content to be

scottish shore

frozen in winter

the north sea

fishing boats with

accompanying gulls

vie for place

a monk gazes out

at the bay of fundy

not dreaming

peaks and valleys

the topography

of a cracked egg

handing back the key

she walks away

and closes the door

in the space

between flower and leaf

a shadow

visiting

foreign countries

on a map

in my bedroom

the music of a cricket

out of tune

cleaning sunfish

the sound of the knife

against bone

polished stones reflect

my wife's personality

beautiful and deep

grumbling thunder

raindrops on water

a small creek

paper birch bark

peels tan under white

reflecting sunrise

beauty

she holds in her hand

a polished stone

purple amethyst

the blue of her eyes

are mine

at the lighthouse

I asked for her hand

in marriage

mainsail set
the boat glides
with the wind

a girl in the lane
as I walk to her
she waits for me

the ship at anchor
small boat brings them ashore
the land moves

my dreams are filled

with the smell of her hair

red gold in sunlight

sitting

cigar smoke curling up

I dream of her

april tenth

still on the lake

thick ice

in the field

the smell of wet earth

takes me back

first green

pushing up

a yellow iris

the cold north sea

all along the watchtower

anemic sun

the grace

of a picture

in minnesota

nosing on the shore

searching for food

a beaver

blackbird plague

an eagle swoops and dives

to escape them

94

kestrel on a wire

making work

of an afternoon

coloraine

the color of rust

out of the ground

pelicans circle

prehistoric birds

nest in trees

noisy forest edge

the debating of turkeys

a feather lost

signing

rapid hand movements

the beauty of words

purple thistle

the flower of scotland

grows wild

random thoughts

producing random haiku

the mind

taken away

from the life I knew

who am I

summer's shadow

on my mind

restless dreams

boiling eggs

the sounds

the water makes

dripping rain

a relentless pursuit

of wetness

fall leaves fall

falling into a fall

they fall

embracing

a new life

all I can do

to cure love's fury

life naturally takes

only what we need

music is surely

what is in between the notes

between you and I

everyone talking

no one knows how to listen

anymore

old ways

grounded in love

come back to me

the spirit moves

within my soul

opening outward

naturally

I open my soul

the spirit speaks

opening

like a flower in spring

my understanding

listening

to the quiet of the night

I hear my voice

misty rain

from a squirrel's twitching tail

anticipation

a breeze

sways leaves of rain

damp earth

to my ears comes

the sound of dripping rain

memories lost

Thank you for reading these haiku.

You can find my blog, "The Window'" at marshallbutcharmstrong.com.

I am on Twitter at:
@butch_armstrong and
@words_breaking

For Facebook search:
Marshall Butch Armstrong

www.ingramcontent.com/pod-product-compliance
Lightning Source LLC
Chambersburg PA
CBHW070642030426
42337CB00020B/4121